Rhythms All Aquiver

Rhythms All Aquiver

Poems by

Barbara Wuest

Cover design by Shay Culligan
Cover photograph by Joan Miller

ISBN: 978-1-952326-56-1

Kelsay Books
502 South 1040 East, A-119
American Fork, Utah, 84003

for Polly and Sandy

When you suffer your sense of rhythm deserts you.
—John O'Donahue

But who has praise enough?
—George Herbert

Acknowledgments

Christianity and Literature: "Chapel of the Stigmata"

First Things: "Stella and Her Late August Garden"

Literal Latte: "Chicago"

2rRiver.org: "The Real World" (w/audio)

The Shepherd Express online: "The Home Team"

Contents

Orchid Garden, Cuba

Hugged by the lush and foreign greenery
we trudged the rugged terrain, rewarded
by strange manifestations of the familiar
flower we'd pinned to our mother's dress
in more Mays than anyone can count:

like the tiger orchid, gentler than its
name-sake, its yellow stripes and five
petals showing off, a puppet without
strings putting herself forward as if
to say look, look at me, just look.

And I do, only to discover at its center
a smaller outgrowth, white, resembling
a ballerina whose legs have become one.
In the puffed sleeves of her costume she
floats, evading my efforts to pin her down,

to say one thing about what goes on between
observers and the wonders that stop us short.
So we add another layer, make up stories,
look to the past, while the royal observed sits
in the corner guarding its secrets as it must.

Traveling

I went. I saw
the blue water splashing
as promised, over the *Malecon*.
It didn't disappoint; the blue was as
true for real as it was on the glossy page.

Like Cuba I am aging, doing what I can

with what's left.

With much trepidation, I flew to her,
thinking of the priest who'd advised
me not to do what I'm inclined to do.

I was inclined to stay home,
not to rub elbows with islanders so
utterly other I was shy in their presence.

Everyone dances in Havana.
Some live hand to mouth and still

they dance and open their arms,
fold me in and loosen my grip on my
tucked-in life, my control in a shambles
and strewn over the sand like lucky stars.

Photograph: *Viterbo, Italy, 2002*

If you were here I would lead you to the room
where the picture hangs. I would ask you to notice
the way the old stone building seems to rise out of
the hillside as if the earth, not man, gave birth to its form.

I'd point to the contrast of textures, how the weathered
roof tiles remind me of an old braided rug crudely woven
and ready for the rag-bag, how it is saved and elevated
by trees exuding nothing but love, nothing as hard as
the old stone of what might have been someone's home
built with much care, a place where you might imagine
yourself looking over the scene, playing the beholder
the old adage says beauty is the in the eye of. She,
who took the picture, must have been standing on a hill,
looking down on the sturdy old home surrounded by trees
I can't name, and deeply green grass, sweetly un-mown and
dotted with flowers so yellow and pale they are barely there.

She who took the picture is Joan. I know her now and knew
her then, when she traveled with her camera, ready to find
everything lovely and true and bring it back home for us
who've not seen Viterbo, ancient city that popes and kings,
weary from battle, took refuge in. I would tell you of all that
I've read of the place where Joan was, looking through her
glasses, and the lens of her camera, unaware you and I might
one day look through the lenses of our glasses, and the glass
in the frame, at what she had to save, to collapse the distance
between then and now, between the crystalline lens of her
eyes and the crystalline lenses of ours. There are layers of glass
and layers of lines, that can take us there, to Viterbo, Italy,
to see what Joan saw, and love what she loves, she who took
the picture and revered every inch of what I want you to see.

Chapel of the Stigmata

Reverend Trinette sang "I Surrender All" and we listened.
Light from windows above her voice made della Robbia's blue
and white glazes look as wet and alive as the bordering seas.

Francesco, as writers assembled your life from pen and mouth
of those you touched, they knew it must add up to much more
than a plan, more than blood on your tunic, more than the nails.

So we traipse through buildings erected for you, this chapel on
the spot where it's said you saw love seep through to your skin.
A mass is in motion now, our bodies are here where yours was.

My grandmother wrote in 1934 in the art of her hand, pencil on
blue lines of a tablet: *I am just about crazy with all this bunch
to feed and nothing to feed them on,* and as proof that hunger's

related to me I keep her letter in a folder by itself to be safe.
The terra cotta altarpiece, 1480, dizzy with symbols, displays
words, carved when the stone was soft, words that were first

in a heart, then on lips, heard, then saved on parchment: *Come,
all you who pass along the way, stop and see if there is any
sorrow like my sorrow,* and every person I know has a wound

somewhere on the body or the heart: at various times we see it,
or we don't, and I wonder what I'm doing this far from home,
sitting in a varnished pew, as lonely for God as I've ever been.

At the top of the cross a pelican sits on a tuft of green, her right
wing aimed at a troubled sun, her left at a sorrow-filled moon.
The stretched necks of her young feed on her breast while baby-

faced angels decorating the arch look on, as engaged in that scene
as I am in the one unfixed: bodies shifting, wood creaking, a man
preaching, a woman singing of the desire to yield, to give it all up.

Ideals abound in settings like this so we picture situations we live.
Resolved to get rid of hesitance, resolved to face all I have feared,
I look at the art, I hear the song, and I breathe the inside air, only to

walk to the waiting bus, unchanged, cool mountain wind turning.
Yet I saw the della Robbia, I heard Trinette's song, add new traces
to the body of connections miles full of time will surely want back.

Greenest of Green, the Trees After Rain

In due time she takes care of herself,
the earth,

as you take care of you, person of any pronoun
so far named
and indelible on the lips of whomever (the object).

Whoever (subject) utters,
whoever utters unfamiliar syllables,

I regard you, earth says, and should you ever fail
to come up short and actually match
with your musings
textures of time and its loamy soil,

then enter, cross over my threshold, sit down
on the grass and allow me to read your palm:

You stand by your dying mother and hold her
hand while you listen to her wanting to be here.

In the reading, I am the one doing the action,
mother the one being acted upon.

It is not the future. Nor are there fortunes
anywhere in sight.

So, of two minds, back and then forth,
rain and then dry,

we take our places in line and no one sees
our personal shift, no one hears.

Summer Silence

I folded laundry, fluffed pillows,
dusted, now I am drawing stick
figures on a page while talking
on the phone with one who says,
"I visited my friend in hospice
this morning, and he only slept.
He would just sleep and breathe."

No one, today, is mowing their
lawn, trimming hedges or even
pounding a nail within hearing.
I am waiting for her to say more.
She doesn't. She connects me to
him and the dread of last things.
And all she can do is breathe.

I don't say anything; she doesn't,
her friend being large between us.
My first memory parades before
me like one last look being born.
Light seeps through the shades.
I am awake between sleeping
parents and waiting to be heard.

Stella and Her Late August Garden

"Get *that* tomato, there, and that one," she
says as she points with her cane and holds
my arm. We have walked the short space from
the back porch to her late August garden,
tomatoes too ripe, yellow-green peppers
in threes bursting through the dry. Doing
as I'm told, I pick the red ones, snap off
the best peppers and set them, one by one,
on the brown grass. If this moment is as
large as it seems right now, I must
surrender it, give up my self to a will
neither mine nor hers, listen when she says
"When Petey was small, we had a summer this
dry. Get *those* peppers." No pause between
what was and what is, she points again. We
turn and walk back. Then, trading my arm
for the porch rail, she says, "I can make it
from here." And now I return, as if I am
not alone, to gather her sweet gifts.

Till Then, 1996

for my sister Polly

Returning from the winery, newly orphaned,
we sang under the influence of a brand new
absence we didn't know we were savoring
there in the front seat where we sat as
the Mills Brothers' voices rose past our
range asserted themselves in our memories
of songs she'd told us he'd liked.

That our mother and father were lovers
is not news yet it seems entirely new,
tonight, in this car where harmonies
sweeten the evening with words like "darling."
Words neither of us can imagine a coal miner
saying to his wife, let alone begging her
to wait, not for the sun to go down or
morning to arrive, but for him. "Please
wait for me," the four crooners say as we
sisters sing along in the night and drive.

We drive through a moment of our own making,
roam with our voices, and somehow we know
something is being born between us, something
in the excruciating slowness of "Till Then."
Then, which is when, because when, which is
now, can only be then after the two of them
leave you to your own devices halfway between
a good laugh and a good cry, the area for
the songs he knew by heart, and then she did.

Near the Trees

They shade and shelter and protect
like fathers.

Made into paper they die to themselves
like mystics.

There are fathers and mystics and mothers.
There are trees.

There is a father, a mystic, a mother in every solitary life.

In an expandable envelope textured to look like leather
and embossed in gold with the words

Valuable Documents

I found a town, a day, and townspeople
on pieces of paper I spread across the kitchen counter.

A man had died and his wife and children survived.
There's a card with a picture of flowers, of doves hovering
over the words *Wife & Children* impersonally typed.

On the back of the card she'd either blotted her lipstick,
or kissed every inch as if planting her own rosy seal.

Two pinholes remain in this florist's tag, proof there'd been
flowers, fragrant and real, and a ribbon or leaf attached.

What's left is her blot or kiss, what's left is a paper card
made from the pulp of individual trees, mixed and cooled,
rolled and cut, to preserve what is lost and force it to mean.

A picture of buttercups leads me to words written by hand
in fountain-pen ink—*God bless you & your little ones*—

I am no longer little, the day is gone, the town's far away.

And "you," dear mother, left us this print, not of your words
but your lips parted in a whisper, red and impossibly close.

Catalina Interior

From a bus 2,000 feet up we can see
the long ruffled skirt of the ocean
drag back and forth across the sand.
To our left is the land with its limits.

We've only our eyesight to carry us,
and Carlos, the driver, who drones
history into a microphone: pots and
bowls unearthed, jewelry, trinkets.
Natives were hard-working, religious.
They found their god in the sun, he says.
We scan for the dead and see nothing
but unwatered grass, an expanse of sky.

Farther in, the ocean out of sight,
strangers together under one roof,
we gaze out windows searching
for ways to connect with the spiked
brown tufts that dot the dry ground.

Vacancy brings illusions, sun-chills.
Its order violent, interior yet open,
trees too sparse to hide the barrens.
On the bus, heads move out of synch.

We soon disembark in the lion-quiet
of the wilderness, walk gingerly so
as not to disturb its audible silence.
Carlos guides us to a wooden fence.
Startled by life-giving signs, we stop!

An Arabian horse named Fidelity
greets us near the gate and a boyish
trainer leads her around the corral.
Her elegance lightens the heavy air.

Then they bring out a newborn
as fragile as death and we all
become one in our loss
for words…

Eco-Fears

That old birch tree keeps being here.
I keep being here, wondering when
it will topple over in a storm, which
way it will fall and expose its roots.

I think of this weary old planet, this
earth, how it carries the burden of
all of its countries, their histories,
their art, their fragile people who

depend on the globe's ability to
stay where it is and hold us up
for the length of our timed lives.
Surely it will stick around, surely

it will continue to support each
beat of our hearts, each breath.
And the birch? Will it stand for
as long as it takes for us to die?

I worry about tired mother earth,
fear she'll give in to the weight
of our neglect, leave the scene
before we know who she truly is.

United States

God knows we try.

Fathom this: plentitude, abundance,

(this is America)

and poverty and hatred
(this too is).

Yet, it sprawls across the inflatable globe.
Kids can point and show where they live.
Small fingers trace its borders wide across
the north, almost a straight line, the eastern,
the southern around Florida, Texas, the west.

One places her thumb over Minot, North Dakota.

Inland. Center.
Dear Young of all stripes,

we implore you, stop this leak.

Otherwise, earth will collapse,
lose its shape, fall at our feet, dis-
appear...

The Young respond: It's hard.
We are using Love's brain
and still the air slips out.

A Version (Upon Reading Duncan's H.D. Book)

She woke before dawn to the same temporal order,
her hand caressing the bare back of a white horse,

caressing and thinking about her father and mother
at the Chicago World's Fair, 1933, holding hands and

hiding their hearts behind a woven veil and changing
their time into a story, laying it bare before the earth.

They did not reject the best the earth could offer, did
not dream or rise to the occasion when the real beauty

strutted out to do her fan-dance, side-show at the fair.
Everywhere they turned, a century of progress stared

them in the face but it's not about them. No. It's you,
incarnate creature issued from two in the midwest

wandering among dancers and hawkers and fans.
America's backyard, the garden, where they saw

they were naked and before they knew it every
breath they drew was charged with meaning.

You had no idea how many verses it would take
so you just plowed forward saving what seemed

to matter most to those two at the Fair loving
their lives, their country, not to mention that

world beneath the stone where misery hides,
where the witch lurks until time to land softly

in a children's book they read to you so many
times you could pick her out of a line-up, that

ornery witch who never took no for an answer.
But still the high mind must labor in matter

and the physical realities of sex and its many
names beneath the surface, hidden in the heart.

Chicago

Farthest was the horizon, then the Lake, Lakeshore Drive, closer
still the zoo, its camels wandering inside the fence, then the
steamed-up glass of the conservatory, and closer still, the windows
of the suite on the 16th floor where two lie together looking as far
as the horizon and back, too tired for love, recalling their ravenous
desire changing to stronger desire, changing again to refinement
that stays a long time, and they wait to be content to remember,
they wait to be content with the tender unknown.

The tender unknown is a place we know, a village hidden at the
city's edge, where questions float without answers because the
people will it that way. Who are we? The oak tree in the park is dy-
ing. Where are we going? Someone on Clover Lane dreams about
forbearance and shows up at the picnic in a sailor suit. What is the
meaning of life? The girl from the projects hits the croquet ball to-
ward the first wicket and it lands aslant of her goal.

Aslant of her goal, she goes to the book full of beautiful words.
Debris, for example. It's all about rubble, litter, broken things. Yet,
saying it forces your mouth into a smile. And try saying bruise.
Your lips form a circle as if you're about to kiss someone. But we
know its meaning doesn't come close to affection. She said this to
her long time lover as they lay on the bed on the 16th floor. Too
high up to see literal debris or the bruise on a stranger's arm, they
spoke of the bruises of their childhoods, the debris of their past.
Debris's not debris, bruise not bruise. It's what living brings us to,
in time.

And, you know, in time, there's the possibility that bruises and debris, in the spiritual sense, are remade into the image and likeness of everything your daily life tells you is over, dead: twilight in a kayak with hours to think about what you owe one another every day. The sweetness of debris, the healing of the bruise—living returns us to these. We gather our debts. We pay things back. We give and receive. Righting the balance with every single breath, we do our part to steady the boat full of decorative words that, time and again, fall prey to the nobler, more naked and gracious "to be"—on the 16th floor, two alone thinking, just that.

At the Movies, an Elegy

for Peter Christensen (1952-2007)

"GOLDEN DOOR at the Downer Theater—I saw it in York—
MASTERPIECE!!!"

So revved up about lives that arrive second-hand
all he can do is shout in bold print,
unaware weeks later he'd be gone.

"Desire," Peter wrote, "just keeps you
caught in this illusion that someday
you'll be complete."

Desire is large, literally, in the immigrant film he loved.

Postcards with coins growing on trees, a giant onion,
chickens fat beyond belief,

enormous carrots floating in milk
and money falling into pockets with the rain.

Desire is quiet then it's not.

The destitute see, they want.
Father and son crawl up the rocks with stones for the bodiless
cross.

The sign they desire arrives. They go and they risk
losing it all for the plenty they don't have

and it takes so long to prepare:
clothes, shoes of dead barons, hats,
belts to be worn in the new land and
mesh with the style of the moneyed class.

My land is new without Peter, empty yet full of all he left behind,
papers galore in boxes upstairs, all of his thinking silenced, un-
done,

as I am undone watching the film so
full of darkness you want to give up.

But I stay, trusting the light will come back and it does.

In an aerial view of the dock,
one crowd morphs into two as the ship pulls away
marking that great divide between the people who stay
and the people who leave.

It is quiet for a long time then the foghorn blasts

too late, too late to turn back!

Confusion, then order then a storm tosses
bodies about until the living look the same
as the dead.

In the end
the immigrants swim for their lives in a river of milk
and in the end
I leave the movie completely unfinished and lost.

Babushka

It's Friday, always Friday.
The women are in church.
It's three o'clock, the hour.

They wish for the sun to go away,
these women in black who kneel
before the pictures that tell their story.

Crying, sniffling into their cotton handkerchiefs,
they close their eyes, see their young selves in whatever country
they'd left—Yugoslavia, Slovenia, Hungary, Croatia—
for this new land that lets them remember
the eternal heartbeat of want.

Displaced persons,
out-of-step everywhere but here
in this chilly, Romanesque church,
they move from station to station like lumbering bears.

They set up shop in my mind back then, and there they have
stayed, rocking back and forth on their knees, keening,

their hair hidden by woolen babushkas tied
in big knots under quivering chins.

When I was young I kept my distance from these women
whose tiny dark eyes, too private for words, forced me to the door.

Now, nearing their age, I want nothing more than to get up close,
listen to their whisperings, supplications to their God who needs

their tears, not for himself but for these living mourners,
who carry on their backs this foreign land, and the ones where
their people remain in graves, too far away.
So often displaced by time's many shifts, I dare now to pray

to be cleansed by their tears that splash on the earth
and affirm my yearning for my father's home town
where I'll take off my scarf and wait for his kiss.

Whole Cloth

A woman in a feed-sack dress
leans over the washboard, her
lover's wool shirt taking in
water and lye soap.

She rubs the cloth up and down
on the corrugated tin.

She sings.

The old elm tree beside the barn
casts a shadow on the grass
near her feet.

He will be home by the first snow.
The shirt is now clean
and dry.

He will bathe in the kitchen.
She will hand him a towel.

Then he will put on the shirt
and swoop her up in his arms
and carry her, marry her.

The shadow of the elm stays.
Promises don't.

Days pass and he doesn't return,

not for her
not for the bare tree
not for the warm wool shirt.

Bag

Thin plastic bag taken by the wind lands
gently on the branch of a leafy birch.

It stays there for days through drizzle and sun.
Father goes to work, mother goes to work,
the kids go to school and it stays.

Soon, everyone has come home.
The bag is still there on the high branch.

The bag has handles someone had slipped their hands through.

Sometime, somewhere, someone put something in,
took something out,
threw the bag down,
or dropped it
and a breeze carried it away.

Chances are the one dwelling on the life of the bag recalls
the time she was driving in the Cotswolds
in a small car
on a narrow road
under an arch of tall trees
and had to stop for the sheep crossing the road.

It took time.
Some stopped.
One nudged the other.
The other nudged back.
One got turned around in the pack.
The big, wooly mass finally made its way.

Wars sizzle below the surface. The poor work without gain.
Meaning arrives and departs.

She leaves for work one morning in June.
The bag is gone from the high branch. She means to look up
but forgets and walks on,
unsteadily toward the street.

Fortuity

The day would surely be the same whether I'd gotten up at five or
not, whether I'd looked out the front window to make sure I was
still on the same street, whether I'd risen, or not.

Only one person is walking his dog out there, one other early riser
who's already assured the earth's in step with the time it needs
to carry out its purpose which is not only to spin but to be infinity's
foundation.

Plans have been made and plans will be made and plans are carried
out and checked off and the little boy found a quarter on the side-
walk, stuck it in his pocket and how could he have known it had
been dropped by a boy his age?

How could he have known its worth was so much less than
its shininess? How could he have known whether or not
his summer day would be as lucky as it was: little boy
skipping down the road gripping his sun-tinged coin.

The Children of Industry

Offspring of Southerners who made their way
north when Goodyear, Goodrich, Seiberling
and General Tire paid a good hourly wage,

we became the children of the East Barberton
Homes who knew nothing beyond sledding
on cardboard, a lid from a ringer washer,
an occasional "real thing" with runners.

We only knew summers, wading ankle-deep
cupping our hands for tadpoles that swam
in the same palms we'd used to shape snowballs
and snowmen we did our best to put a face on.

Our time had not been divided by anything more
than the state of the creekwater and the length
of the grass we'd push the wickets through
for the glory of the cannonball: heavy and wooden,
touching, mallet lined up, one foot holding our own
down—smack! and the opponent's ball sails

far from the pole striped red, yellow, blue, brown,
black, orange and green. You know your color
is there and you know it's the very pole the rules
require you to hit before you can even think about
winning or being first, before you can even dream.

The Real World

Just when you think you've been on this earth too long
something happens to make it all brand new—a made

thing or persons born, like the woman over there bundled
against the cold walking from the side door toward the

barn that just might collapse if the wind picks up, how
she and the landscape remind you of the character and

setting offered in that novel you read with its affairs,
secrets, suspicious deaths, all seen through the eyes of a

boy who is now a grown man recalling having seen too
much back in those days when his father did wrong with

the woman from the farm who fried the boy some eggs
on the very same day and arrived in his dreams that night.

There's the book, there's the life, there's the thing that
saves, an email, say, sent to your address saying your

best friend fell in love with a man who studies plants
and she is no longer lonely or sad, and just below, in

your inbox, a niece writes in cyberspace in a parrot's
voice, one she made up and assigned a human name,

Ronald, and a country of birth, the moderate UK, alas!
We have a formal exchange in which he pokes fun at

our ways of staying in touch (email offends his soul)
and wonders about a species that hangs onto a distance

he has to relearn, spreading his claws over lettered
keys that "fly" him to Brazil to set the record straight.

What Little Eyes See

Amor eterno, the mariachi sang in their tongue; I didn't get
the words yet the sadness was clear, and soon I heard a voice trans-
lating in my ear:

"Love eternal and unforgettable,
sooner or later I will be with you."

I turned around surprised and he went on, trailing after the singers:
"And even though tranquil is my conscience,
I could have done more."

My translator continued addressing someone's beloved dead:
"How I wish that you lived, that your little eyes had never closed."

Was it a child? I wanted to ask. Is the ballad addressing a child?
But the man disappeared in the crowd and the band shifted to
a happy song. The bride and groom danced and all the people
danced non-stop for hours.

Little eyes, never close, never close, I prayed.

All the tables in the room had cream-colored skirts tied with ribbon
and lace. Yellow paper bells hung from the lights. The dance floor
was glossy and large. Smartly-dressed teens shook their hips,
grown-ups swayed far from all pain and the children skated across
the room in their socks, as *amor eterno,* eternal love

kicked up its heels.

The Home Team

They're so far behind we're stunned.

Chips, dip, cheese, bottles of dark beer.
The eyes of the wolfhound in shadow.

A vantage point: I sit in this chair and
wonder where they came from, who
sent them here, Judith, Carl, Nancy,
Fred, Cheryl, Scotty, Glen, the lovable
Kienan who is three, jumping on my lap
at half-time, reciting an American poem:

"The woods are lovely, dark and deep,"
each word for him a delightful surprise.

He wins. And the wolfhound makes
her way to the chip-dip bowl, her nose
now white as the snow, seeming to think
we will not see her standing there…

It's early November and there's only
rain and fierce, fierce wind, the Lake
a short walk east roaring like the ocean.
"Jesus H. Christ!" Scotty rails at the tv.
Wind howls down the quiet street.

Anything could happen, the last brown
leaves torn from the trees, swirl under
the lights. They can't land. Night just is.
I try to resist its eternal, willowy sway.

The wistful eyes of the dog appear
in a doorway that looks like the posts
and lintels of so many goals gone awry.
It's about winning, winning, says Vince.

I mean *said.* Lombardi *said,* and fierce
winds telling me there is time for breath,

for taking a deep one the people close by
never need to know is theirs, and for them.

Figure in a Winter Scene

A woman is saying goodbye to a man
who sits at a table reading the news.

She pulls on her gloves.
She wraps the woolen scarf around her neck
and says to the reading man:

"I wish there was a way to quell what's drawing me
past this room and out toward the whistling woods
where I hear there are answers…"

Suddenly, she spots an owl, its stillness all chesty proud.

The man looks where she's looking.
They are staring at the owl
at the edge of the snow-filled yard

and scanning their memories for tales
they'd heard about wisdom and death
and which to believe *this* one would bring and when.

Snow falls over last night's snow.
Dawn pulls back
from the encroachment of day.

Minutes pass. The owl has not moved.

There at the edge of the yard it is frozen
in place: a still life with owl, wood chips,
and the lowest branch of a dark green pine.

"The only thing moving is the snow," he says.
"Everything receives it but the owl," she says.

Luck

Our city is civilized.
Lawns, flowers, receptacles for waste,
we keep things pretty and tame.

Then one morning you see from your window a fox
lying on the soft green grass gnawing the night's
find—

you've read of a bear mangling a man out of his life
somewhere in Montana's wilds

it's noon of the same day
the fox and its prey are gone

yet the soft grass is filled with their absence

from the second floor you look down on the yard
where the fox had devoured the smaller one

it's an old story, an old wonder

we go to zoos, we whale-watch
become these creatures, some beautiful, some vile

some beautiful *and* vile as the fox was with his reddish
brown coat and long long tail moving in the air as he ate
and you watched as giddily horrified as you've ever been

Before the sun goes down, you stroll across the grass
and find among the blades the foot of a rabbit you
shove in a bag then toss into the bin
marked *trash*.

Rooting Around

in memory of Zbigniew Sorbjan

A lessening lingers up and down our street.
My aunts would have said it was *his time.*
It's ours too, we who still wait, write emails,
plan meals and wonder anew what it means.

At one neighborhood new year's event,
he read the Polish and I read the English
translation of Wislawa Szymborska's poem
"Cat in an Empty Apartment" and, as we

prepared, he told me which lines were not
quite rendered correctly in my language.
But I read them as they were on the page:
"Footsteps on the staircase...not the same."

Sympathetic listeners heard both ways
of saying what the speaker wants to know
about the cat, the space, and countries old
and new searching for the words for how

absence is received by an owner's pet,
who's clearly at a loss, checking the
closets, the shelves, the bowl with no
fish, no lamps lit as they used to be.

The Way of the Body

Mine is sometimes too present, too much
on my mind, the way it feels, the way it
looks, the way it leads me in directions
I may or may not want to go now or ever.

It is said the body and soul are one and
the same but I really don't see it that way.
I can easily forget my soul is around but
my body badgers me day in and day out.

It needs this, it needs that, it's tired, it's
restless, it's hungry for food or for love.
Even in sleep it fidgets and moans, rolls
this way then that in search of its timid

little soul that hides behind the drapes,
peeks out every so often looking for a
clearing that will help it to bolster my
flesh in its quest for union and rest.

All Aquiver

Afternoons to be
gotten through
come alive

when I summon
my demons
without fear.

Only then
—all aquiver—
do I wake.

Only then
do I reach
the source

that explains
the illogical
nature of truth,

how it swells
at first hearing
and shoves away

the geometry
my life has been
trapped in since

day one, day two,
gathering at last
with the tenderest

three
and then three
then the holiest three.

Ah, Guests

All summer long we receive
them who are us in disguise
after awhile and we become

blood related, sleeping in one
house as we do, them and us.
Surprised at the breakfast table

that we are being this blessed,
we—them and us—hold back
the ahh we'd say if we let go,

the ahhh we would say softly
were we to sink into a pool
after hours in the good sun.

We need our sweet guests,
want them too, every last
one which keeps us two

going strong through silent
afternoons with no time to
lose not one second, not two,

alert as we are to days past
when the loved were too far
away to hug or be our third.

Childless

What's it like?
Footsteps in the night the carpet buffers
go away, go away, go away, go away.

Well, yes, it haunts a woman
and man: Ancestors clamoring to be
manifest in sex and out, incessant,

the world's infinite unborn
being contained, civilized potential
stirring in bedrooms from Irvine to Milwaukee,

from Dayton to London, from where
we were to where we would
always go, and try and try
as we might the forever not-yet

of the effort to take like a picture, to develop
like a roll of film lost in a tube
we are sure is somewhere, somewhere.

Perspective

"If you stand on the earth
you can't see the earth,"
the young girl said.

Of course. No question.
The logic is simple, clear.

You are twelve, like the girl.

You can't see yourself
standing in the large field,
not a tree in sight, only
willowy wheat, swaying.

You are wearing a sleeveless
dress on a day too humid
for shoes.

Twilight after wrestling
the wet air, you are seized
by what you think you see
in the coming light, unaware
your feet impose limits

as you pivot, unable
to look down, or back,
unable to stop.

The Unbuilt

In search of shelter, a house of her
own, the poor widow shuffled across
the spring-green grass and suddenly
tripped over a yellow metal beam.

She had seen the large cranes in the city
swinging gray beams over an unfinished
building, layer by layer, joining one floor
to the next, trying to make things whole.

When she was a child she dreamed
a house into being; over and over
she'd lay out the square foundation
with red-tip matches made of wood.

Turning over, her back on the grass,
facing the evening sky, she saw four
colorful beams reaching toward one
another, aiming forever to connect.

(Inspired by Forrest Myers' sculpture *Quartet*)

Thou

art the last resort

(I'm afraid)

that's how weak my faith

yet, you are ever open to doubt

self- and otherwise you are open

I say yes I'm ready and you draw

nearer and nearer and I say

not you but Thou

repeat ancient word, distance

protecting me from having to

concede and change and address

You art

Notes

"Traveling": The Malecon is the stone embankment alongside the waterfront in Havana.

"Photograph: *Viterbo, Italy, 2002*": The photograph was taken by Joan Miller, photographer, Milwaukee, Wisconsin.

"Chapel of the Stigmata": "I Surrender All" is a Christian hymn written by Judson W. Van DeVenter (American, 1855-1939); it was put to music by Winfield S. Weeden (American, 1847-1908). When I was at the Chapel, I heard it sung by Reverend Trinette McCray, Baptist minister, Milwaukee, Wisconsin.

"Chapel of the Stigmata": This chapel is located in La Verna, Italy, built on the spot where it is believed that St. Francis received the stigmata. In the Christian tradition, the stigmata refers to the appearance of bodily wounds on the hands or feet that correspond to the crucifixion wounds of Jesus Christ.

"Chapel of the Stigmata": Andrea della Robbia (1435-1525) was a leading sculptor during the Italian Renaissance. He was known for his expertise in the use of glazed terra cotta for his sculptures.

"A Version": *The H.D. Book.* Robert Duncan, University of California Press, 2011.

"Till Then, 1996": The song "Till Then" was written by Eddie Seiter, Sol Marcus and Guy Wood. The Mills Brothers recorded it in 1944 and made it a hit. I was born in 1946. My father would have sung this song in our living room for us to hear. He died, unexpectedly, in 1954 when he was 33.

"At the Movies, an Elegy": "Golden Door," written and directed by Emanuele Cralese in 2006, is about a family that migrates from rural Italy to Ellis Island in New York City at the beginning of the 20th century. Lured to the land they know only from postcards showing America as a place where everything is rich and absurdly large, including the carrots, the Italian peasants scrounge around for things that they think will help them to fit in, shoes and hats of dead barons, for example. The voyage and the arrival are not easy, the door not so golden after all. My brilliant friend, Peter, would have identified with the peasants. He died unexpectedly and too young. It was as if a very important door had slammed shut in my face. We were not finished being friends. I was not finished learning from him.

"The Children of Industry": East Barberton Homes is the name of the housing projects in Barberton, Ohio, where I grew up after my father died when I was seven.

"What Little Eyes See": The song "Amor Eterno" was written by Mexican composer Juan Gabriel but was first released by singer Rocio Durcal (Madrid). Though urban legend says the song is about Durcal's son who died in an accident, Gabriel actually wrote the song to honor his mother who died. Since the song is about love and loss, it is often heard at weddings (where I first heard it) as well as funerals.(wearemitu.com/entertainment/amor-eterno-song-love-loss)

"Perspective": The young girl I heard these words from is Neera Maz.

"The Unbuilt": Forrest Myers' sculpture, *Quartet,* is located on the grounds of the Lynden Sculpture Garden in Milwaukee, Wisconsin.

About the Author

Barbara Wuest, a graduate of UC-Irvine's MFA in Creative Writing, taught English and Creative Writing at Cardinal Stritch University in Milwaukee. Her poems have appeared in a variety of literary journals such as *The Cape Rock, Wind Literary Journal, Western Ohio Journal, Laurel Review, The Paris Review, Cincinnati Poetry Review, Dogwood, CrossCurrents, Oberon, The Beloit Poetry Journal, Wisconsin Academy Review* and others. She served as a poetry editor for the *Association of Franciscan Colleges and Universities (AFCU) Journal. Among Others,* a chapbook of poetry, was published by *Finishing Line Press* (2015). Her poetry collection, *Shadowy Third*, was published by Aldrich Press (2016). *Monarchs Fly Great Distances,* a poetry collection, was published by Aldrich Press (2018). She also published a memoir, *Drive Gently,* (2017). Barbara and her husband Glen live in Milwaukee.

www.ingramcontent.com/pod-product-compliance
Lightning Source LLC
Chambersburg PA
CBHW071358090426
42738CB00012B/3157